Understanding My Emotions

When I'm Overwhelmed

Understanding My Emotions

When I'm Angry
When I'm Embarrassed
When I'm Happy
When I'm Lonely
When I'm Overwhelmed
When I'm Sad
When I'm Scared
When I'm Sorry
When I'm Surprised
When I'm Worried

Understanding My Emotions

When I'm Overwhelmed

ALEXANDRA DALTON

**Understanding My Emotions
When I'm Overwhelmed**

Copyright © 2016 by Village Earth Press, a division of Harding House Publishing. All rights reserved. No part of this publication may be reproduced or transmitted in any form or by any means, electronic or mechanical, including photocopying, recording, taping, or any information storage and retrieval system, without permission from the publisher.

Village Earth Press
Vestal, New York 13850
www.villageearthpress.com

First Printing
9 8 7 6 5 4 3 2 1

Series ISBN (paperback): 978-1-62524-440-6
ISBN (paperback): 978-1-62524-380-5
ebook ISBN: 978-1-62524-136-8
   Library of Congress Control Number: 2014944104

Author: Dalton, Alexandra.

Contents

To the Teacher or Parent 7

When I'm Overwhelmed 8

Find Out More 42

Feeling Words 44

Index 46

Picture Credits 47

About the Author 48

To the Teacher or Parent

More than a hundred years ago, John Dewey insisted that the true purpose of schooling was not simply to teach children a trade but to train them in deeper habits of mind. Social-emotional learning builds on Dewey's theory further, suggesting that emotional skills are crucial to both academic performance and future success in life.

The research is definitive: emotional training is good for children! A recent study, reported in the *New York Times*, found that preschoolers who had even a single year of social-emotional training continued to perform better two years after they left the program; they were less aggressive and less anxious than children who hadn't participated in the program. Another study found that K-12 students who received some form of emotional instruction scored an average of 11 percentile points higher on standardized achievement tests. A similar study found a nearly 20 percent decrease in students' violent behaviors.

The goal of this series of books, UNDERSTANDING MY EMOTIONS, is to instill in young children a foundation of emotional intelligence. Use these books to help your students learn to understand, identify, and regulate their emotions. Give them important tools that will serve them well for the rest of their lives!

When I'm

OVERWHELMED

Every day, I have lots of feelings going on inside me. They're called emotions. Some emotions feel good. Some emotions feel scary or sad. And sometimes, my emotions feel just too big.

When that happens, I don't know how to handle my feelings. It feels likes my emotions are yelling so loud inside me, I can't hear anything else. I wish I could just plug my ears and make the feelings go away. But I can't!

I feel overwhelmed!

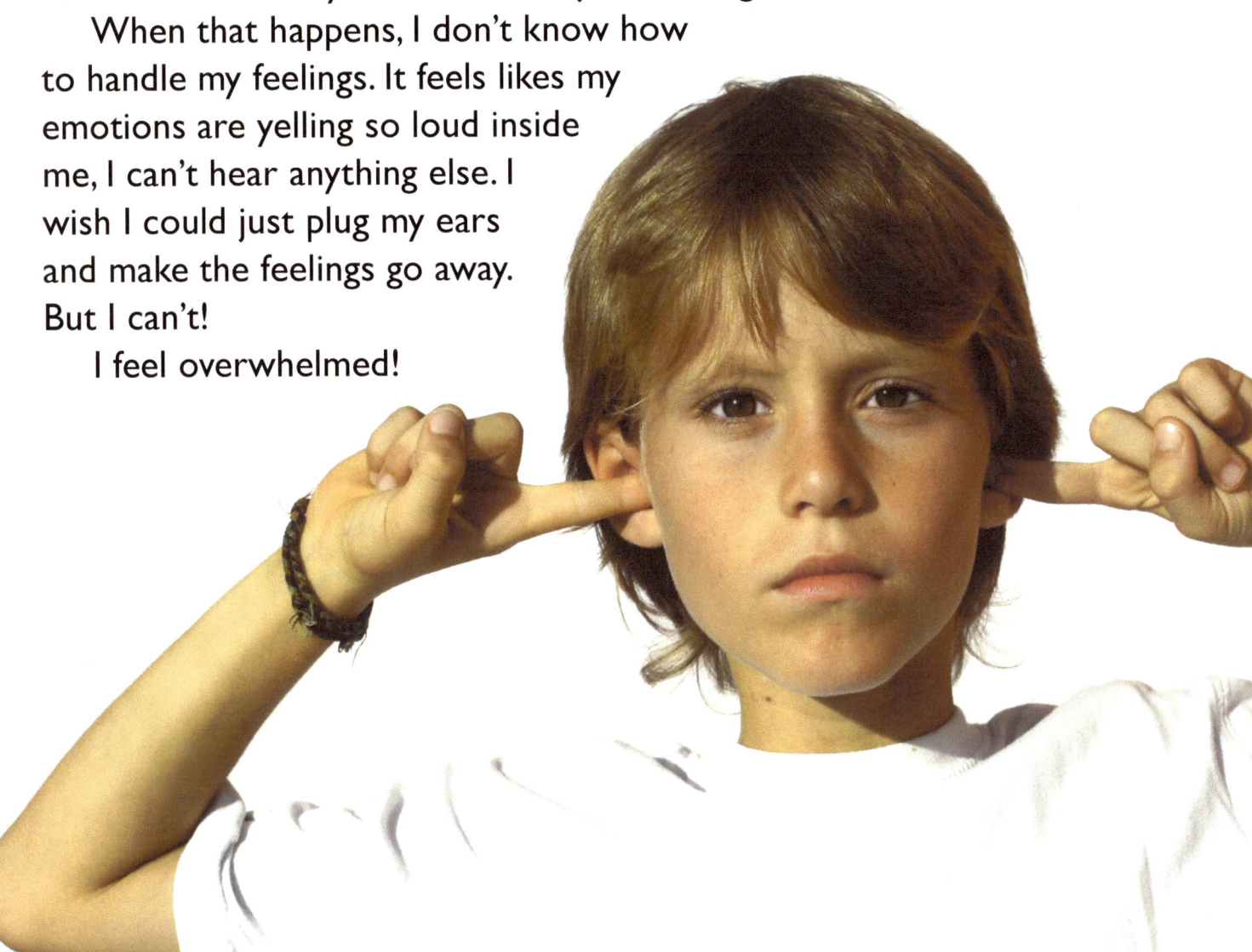

Everybody has emotions. They come and they go every day.

Sometimes people feel happy . . .

and other times people feel sad.

Sometimes people feel angry.

Other times people feel scared.

Sometimes people feel like laughing . . .

and sometimes people want to cry.

Sometimes people just feel overwhelmed! They don't know how to cope with their emotions!

Lots of things change the way I feel. Other people can do things that change my emotions. They can make me feel glad or sad.

I feel happy when I'm having fun with my dad.

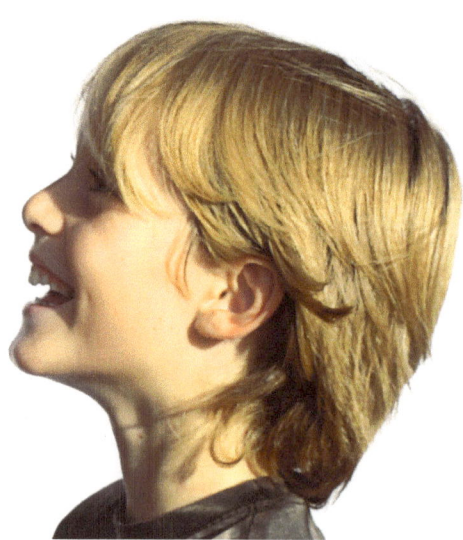

But I don't feel happy when he yells at me! When my dad is angry with me, I feel sad. Sometimes I feel scared. And sometimes when my dad is angry, I feel angry too!

Sometimes all those feelings just pile up. When my dad is angry on the same day that I get teased at school, it feels like too much. I'm already upset about my dad, and then I get upset all over again because some kid is mean to me.

Maybe it's not really such a big deal—but it FEELS like a big deal. When I'm overwhelmed, everything just feels like more than I can handle!

Other things make me feel overwhelmed too. Yesterday, my grandpa and grandma had a big argument.

And then I had to go for my swimming class. Usually, I think swimming class is fun, but this time, I was already upset about my grandparents' fight. And then I felt nervous because my swimming teacher wanted me to try something new. It was just too much. I felt overwhelmed!

When I got home from swimming class, I was still feeling upset. All my emotions were jumping around inside me. I could hardly think!

So when my sister asked me a question, I turned around and yelled at her. I knew it wasn't her fault I was feeling so overwhelmed. But my feelings seemed too big to keep inside!

Then my grandma told my sister and me to go wash her car. At first, I didn't want to do it. It felt like one more thing on top of everything else.

But my grandma said that if I got busy and thought about something else, it would help me not feel so overwhelmed. And she was right! Pretty soon, my sister and I were laughing. I didn't feel overwhelmed anymore.

Later that night, my grandma and I talked some more. She said that everyone feels overwhelmed sometimes. Even grownups! Grownups have the same feelings kids do. Grownups feel happy and sad, angry and scared.

And sometimes, grownups get overwhelmed!

Grownups can feel overwhelmed when they're too busy. When too many things are happening all at once, they don't know how to cope with all their feelings. They're not so different from kids! Sometimes adults call this overwhelmed feeling STRESS.

Feelings are going on inside people all the time. Emotions take place INSIDE people.

But I can tell what people are feeling by the way they look on the OUTSIDE. Their faces, voices, and bodies give me clues.

I can tell when other people feel happy because they smile more. They laugh. Their voices sound happy. The crinkly little lines around their eyes tell me they're happy.

I can also tell when people are feeling sad and angry by looking at their faces and listening to their voices. If I pay attention, even the way people move tells me about their inside feelings.

When people are sad, angry, or upset, their mouths might turn down at the corners.

Angry people sometimes cross their arms in front of them. Their shoulders might slump, and they might put their heads down. They might put their hands over their faces.

27

People act different ways when they're overwhelmed. Sometimes people who are feeling overwhelmed use loud voices—but not always. Sometimes when people are overwhelmed they get really quiet. When I feel overwhelmed, sometimes I just want to be all by myself. I want people to leave me alone.

Other times, I forget about my troubles by doing something fun. I go outside and play . . .

or I draw a picture . . .

or I put on headphones and listen to music . . .

or I play with my dog.

Lots of things can help me feel better. My grandma says she likes to exercise when she's feeling overwhelmed with life. She says I should try it too!

I try different things to help me cope when I feel overwhelmed. Sometimes just acting silly helps!

My grandma says it's important to listen to my feelings. They're messages that say, "Pay attention! Notice what's going on!"

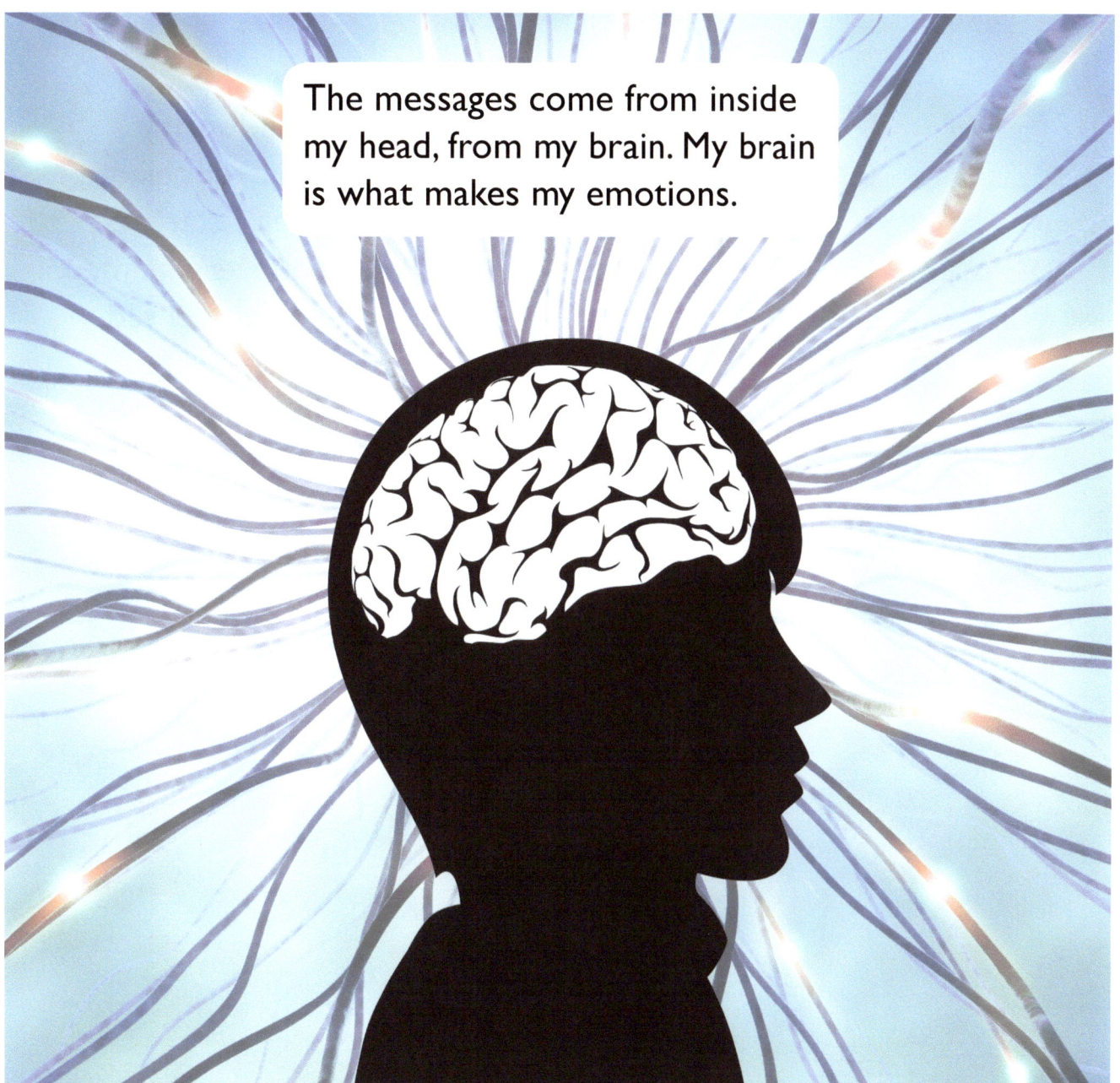

When I pay attention, my brain will tell me when I start to feel overwhelmed. I might feel sad—or I might get angry easier than I usually would. When I know what's going on, I can do something to change the situation.

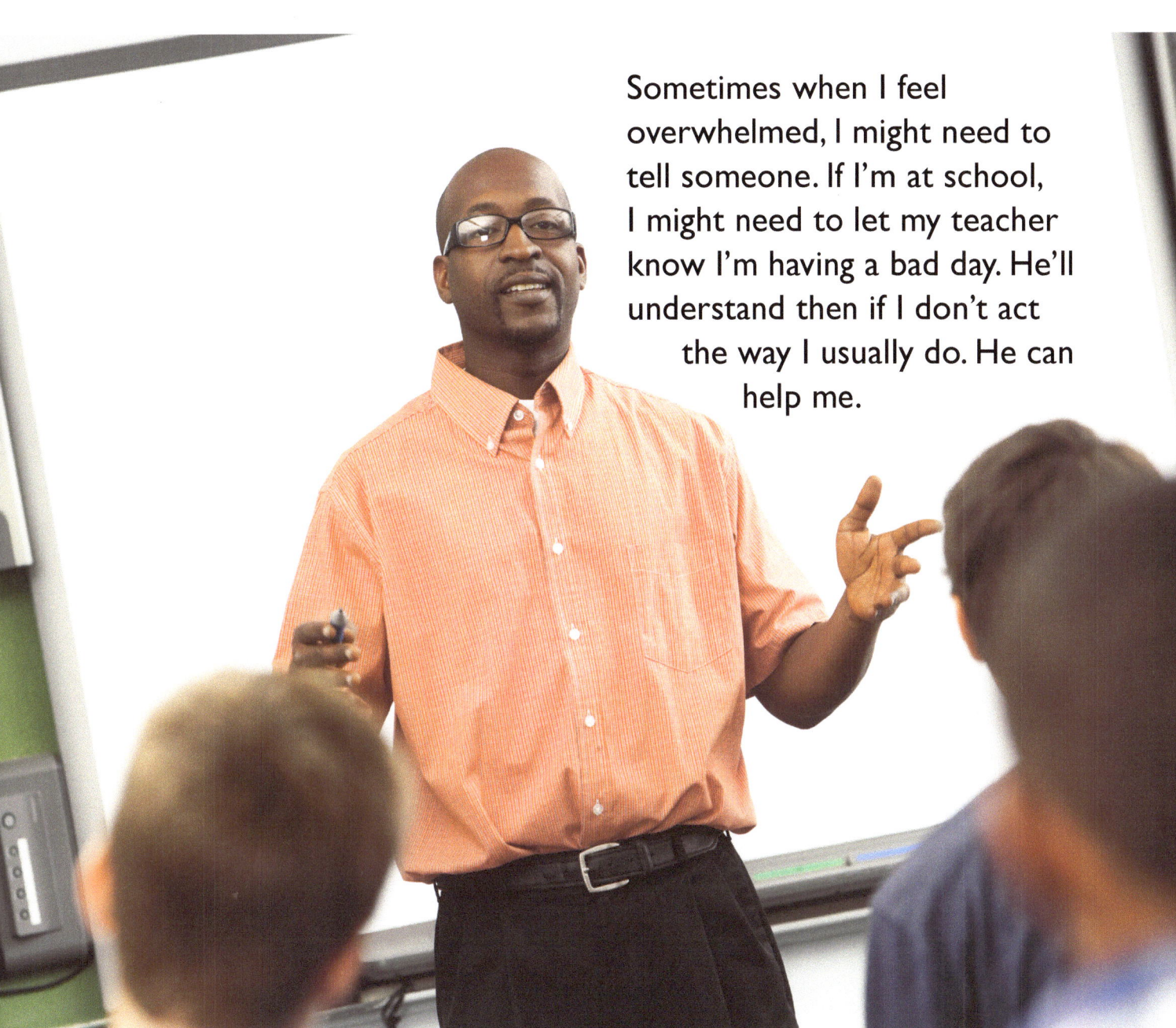

Sometimes when I feel overwhelmed, I might need to tell someone. If I'm at school, I might need to let my teacher know I'm having a bad day. He'll understand then if I don't act the way I usually do. He can help me.

I can also tell my friends when I'm feeling overwhelmed. They might be able to tell by my face and voice—but it's even better if I use my words to let them know what I'm feeling. Real friends will understand.

I can pay attention to what my friends and family are feeling, too. I can notice when they are feeling overwhelmed. When they are, I can ask them what I can do to help.

I can be careful not to bother them. I don't want to add more stress to their lives! Maybe they need a smile—or a hug. Maybe they just need to be left alone.

My grandpa says when he feels overwhelmed, he just wants to plug his ears so he can't hear anything that's going on. I understand how he feels!

One of my teachers says when she feels overwhelmed, she gets a headache. She says she gets angry easier with her students when she feels like that! When I understand how she's feeling, I can find ways to help her by giving her a smile and listening to her carefully while she's talking.

Everyone feels overwhelmed once in a while. Sometimes, life seems just too hard to handle. On the next page are some things you can try the next time you feel overwhelmed.

- find something that makes you laugh.
- get busy doing something else.
- spend some time alone.
- do something fun.
- take a nap.
- ask someone for help.

Most of all, be patient. Feeling overwhelmed never lasts forever. Soon you'll feel better!

Find Out More

You can learn more about your emotions by going online and checking out these websites. Some of the sites have videos you can watch or games you can play. You could also read the other books in this series to find out more about feelings—or you could go to your library and see if you can find the books listed on the next page. There's a lot more you can learn about loneliness and other feelings!

On the Internet

It's My Life: Emotions
pbskids.org/itsmylife/emotions

KidsHealth: Feelings
kidshealth.org/kid/feeling

Model Me: Faces and Emotions
www.modelmekids.com/emotions_dvd.html

In Books

Cook, Julia. *The Worst Day of My Life Ever!* Boys Town, NE: Boys Town Press, 2011.

Lamia, Mary C. *Understanding Myself: A Kid's Guide to Intense Emotions and Strong Feelings.* Washington, DC: Magination, 2010.

Lite, Lori. *Bubble Riding: A Relaxation Story.* Marietta, GA: Stress Free Kids, 2008.

———. *Sea Otter Cove.* Marietta, GA: Stress Free Kids, 2008.

McCloud, Carol. *Have You Filled a Bucket Today? A Guide to Daily Happiness for Kids.* Northville, MI: Ferne Press, 2006.

Wilde, Jerry. *Hot Stuff to Help Kids Chill Out.* Richmond, IN: LGR, 2003.

Williams, Mary. *Cool Cats, Calm Kids: Stress Management for Young People.* Atascadero, CA: Impact, 2007.

Feeling Words

Overwhelmed is just one of the words we use when we talk about feelings. But there are many more words that describe feelings. Here are some of those words.

Excited

Angry

Embarrassed

Worried

Guilty

Hurt

Proud

Scared

Shy

Sorry

Surprised

Bored

Index

An index is a way you can quickly find something inside a book. The numbers tell you exactly what page to go to if you want to find that word.

alone 28, 37, 41
angry 10, 13–14, 20, 26–27, 34, 39
arm 27

bodies 23
brain 33–34
busy 19, 21, 41

cope 11, 21, 31
cry 11

dad 12–14
dog 29

ear 9, 38
exercise 30
eyes 24

face 23, 26–27, 36
fight 17
friends 36–37

fun 12, 17, 29, 41

glad 12
grandma 16, 19–20, 30, 32
grandpa 16, 38

hands 27
happy 10, 12–13, 20, 24
head 27, 33
hug 37

laugh 24, 41

mouth 26
music 29

nap 41

patient 41
picture 29
play 29

quiet 28

sad 9–10, 12–13, 20, 26, 34
scared 11, 13, 20
scary 9
school 14, 35
shoulders 27
silly 31
sister 18–19
smile 24, 37, 39
stress 21, 37

teacher 17, 35, 39
trouble 29

upset 14, 17–18, 26

voice 23–24, 26, 28, 36

words 36

Picture Credits

p. 8: © Godfer | Dreamstime.com
p. 9: © Godfer | Dreamstime.com
p. 10: © Godfer | Dreamstime.com, © Yael Weiss | Dreamstime.com
p. 11: © Yael Weiss | Dreamstime.com (all images)
p. 12: © Godfer | Dreamstime.com
p. 13: © Godfer | Dreamstime.com
pp. 14-15: © Godfer | Dreamstime.com
p. 16: © Waxart | Dreamstime.com
p. 17: © Godfer | Dreamstime.com
p. 18: © Godfer | Dreamstime.com
p. 19: © Godfer | Dreamstime.com
p. 20: © Tan Wei Ming | Dreamstime.com, © Hongqi Zhang (aka Michael Zhang) | Dreamstime.com, © Spaxia | Dreamstime.com, © Phovoir | Dreamstime.com
p. 21: © Jaim924 | Dreamstime.com
p. 22: © Marcel De Grijs | Dreamstime.com
p. 23: © Marcel De Grijs | Dreamstime.com
p. 24: © Jason Stitt | Dreamstime.com
p. 25: © Canettistock | Dreamstime.com, © Leung Cho Pan | Dreamstime.com, © Spotmatik | Dreamstime.com, © Miroslav Ferkuniak | Dreamstime.com
p. 26: © Herman Lumanog | Dreamstime.com, © Aspenphoto | Dreamstime.com, © Lapetitelumiere | Dreamstime.com
p. 27: © Pavlo Lysenko | Dreamstime.com, © Photographerlondon | Dreamstime.com, © Limalo58 | Dreamstime.com
p. 28: © Godfer | Dreamstime.com
p. 29: © Godfer | Dreamstime.com, © Elena Schweitzer | Dreamstime.com, © Micaela Sanna | Dreamstime.com, © Yaro75 | Dreamstime.com
p. 30: © Waxart | Dreamstime.com
p. 31: © Godfer | Dreamstime.com
p. 32: © Pflpitation | Dreamstime.com
p. 33: © Dmstudio | Dreamstime.com
p. 34: © Godfer | Dreamstime.com
p. 35: © Monkey Business Images | Dreamstime.com
p. 36: © Jose Manuel Gelpi Diaz | Dreamstime.com
p. 37: © Saša Prudkov | Dreamstime.com
p. 38: © Waxart | Dreamstime.com
p. 39: © Imagevillage | Dreamstime.com
p. 40: © Yael Weiss | Dreamstime.com, © Dejan Jovanovic | Dreamstime.com
p. 41: © Godfer | Dreamstime.com
p. 44: Fotolia: © Fasphotographic, © Cantor Pannato, © Andres Rodriguez, © Gabriel Blaj, © Moodboard Premium, © Halfpoint
p. 45: Fotolia: © Cantor Pannato, © Blend Images, © Zhekos, © Olly, © Wavebreak Media Micro; © Serrnovik | Dreamstime.com

About the Author

Alexandra Dalton was a teacher, and now she is a writer. When she was a teacher, she helped her students talk about their feelings. She knows that it's hard work sometimes to talk about our feelings—but she knows we feel better and we get along with each other better when we can use our words to talk about how we feel. Alexandra has three children. She also has a dog and a cat and four goats. She lives in New York State.

www.ingramcontent.com/pod-product-compliance
Lightning Source LLC
Chambersburg PA
CBHW061359090426
42743CB00002B/70